CONTENTS

CHAPTER 1: INTRODUCTION

Skydiving gives a feeling of total freedom. People jump from an aircraft and fall freely. Then they open their parachutes and float back to Earth.

SKYDIVING

by Lesley Gale

The author

Lesley Gale has been skydiving for 23 years and has made over 3,500 jumps, and won six British and 11 world records. She has won over 100 skydiving medals, including two European golds, three European silvers and a world bronze. Lesley has organized the last three British women's records.

With thanks to: Hayley Terry, Diana LeCore and Anna Brett

Thank you to Lorraine Petersen and the members of nasen

ISBN-13: 978 1 84898 140 9 pbk
This revised edition published in 2010 by *ticktock* Media Ltd

Printed in China
9 8 7 6 5 4 3 2 1

A CIP catalogue record for this book is available from the British Library.

First published in Great Britain as *Xtreme Sports* in 2008 by *ticktock* Media Ltd,
103 Goods Station Road, Tunbridge Wells, Kent, TN1 2DP

Picture credits (t=top; b=bottom; c=centre; l=left; r=right; OFC=outside front cover):
Erik Aasbarg: 45b. Airbourne Systems: 13t. Airtec: 21t. Alti-2: 21c. Chris Barry/Action Plus: 24t. Felix Baumgartner: 54. Hans Berggren: 21b, 37b. Bettmann/Corbis: 11cl. Darren Birkin: 35b. Fiona Birnie: 41t. Willy Boeykens: 2, 6b, 14/15, 18t, 33t, 34/35t, 36, 41b. Bone Head: 18b. J C Colclasure: 27t. Rob Colpus: 60b. Corbis: 10t. Tony Danbury: 47t. Jay Epstein: 55b. F.A.I.: 60b. Andy Ford: 25c, 49t. Oliver Furrer: 53tr. Sarah Hall: 38b, 39br. Mark Harris: 32t, 57t. Tony Hathaway: 42/43. Richard Hayden: 29bl. Ian (Milko) Hodgkinson: 59t. Ash Hollick: 47b. Simon Hughes: 46. iStock: OFC background. Jump Shop: 19t. Jupiter Images/Thomas Ulrich: 55t. Norman Kent: 7b, 22/23, 29br, 56. Keith MacBeth: 28/29t. Peter Male: 48. Anton Malevsky: 28b. Michael McGowan: 30/31. Neil McLaren: 13b. Mike Mumford: 11tr. Francisco Neri: 16/17t, 26t, 27cl, 40t. Craig O'Brian: 37t, 52t. Dean O'Flaherty: 4/5, 6/7t, 44/45t. Johnny Panakis: 58. Patrick Passe: 53cl. Jason Peters: 40b. Photolibrary: 1, 33c. Grant Richards: 61b. Shutterstock: OFC (skydiver), 3, 20, 50/51. Sky High Entertainment Movies: 59b. Barbara Sokol/Beck Isle Museum/Sydney Smith: 9b. Square One: 19cr. James Stevenson: 38/39t. Jack Sullivan/Alamy: 17b. *ticktock* Media Archive: 25t. Total Control: 19bl. Gary Wainwright: 16b, 34b, 44b. Simon Ward, sward@airkix.com: 49b, 57b. Wikipedia: 8t, 9t.

OVERVIEW

Skydiving means diving into the sky from an aircraft, helicopter or balloon. There are two types: free falling and parachuting.

The parachute is also called the canopy.

Parachuting

After the free fall, it is time to open the parachute. This part of the jump is called parachuting.

Mental aspects

You need to be brave to jump out of an aircraft.

Skydiving builds confidence.

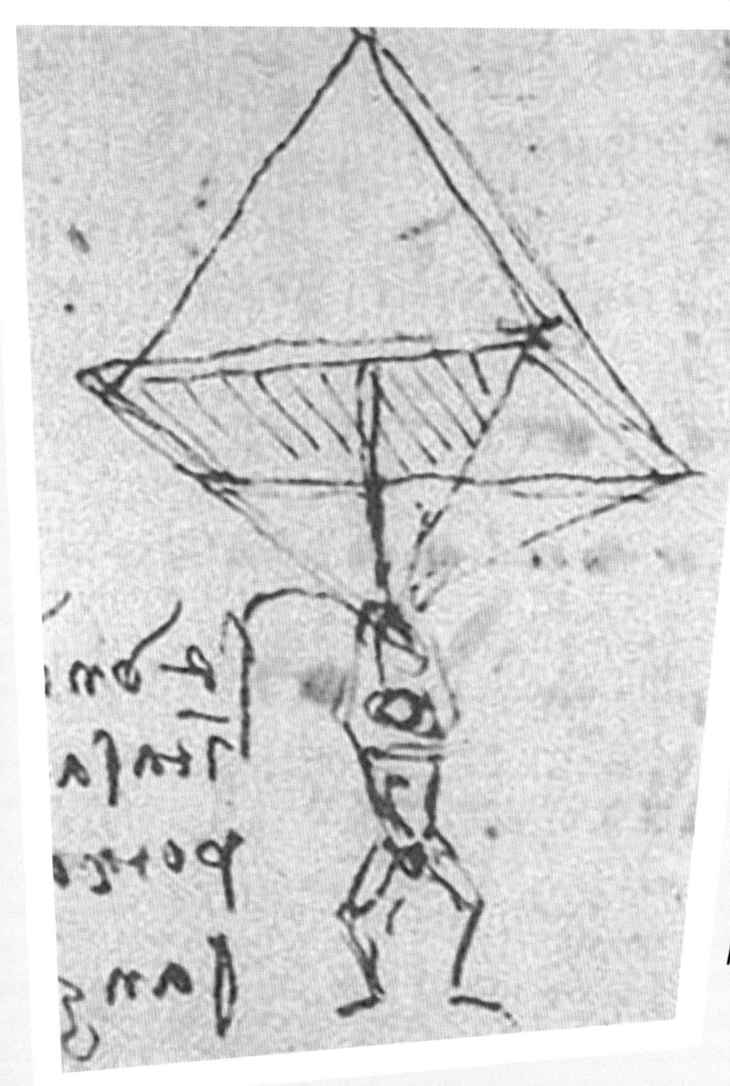

Leonardo da Vinci's parachute sketch (1483)

EARLY HISTORY

Parachuting began in the 15th century when Italian Leonardo da Vinci sketched a parachute in his notebook.

Leonardo's parachute was made of cloth over a pyramid-shaped frame. His idea was to help people to escape from burning buildings.

Sébastien Lenormand parachuting from the Montpelier Observatory in 1783

Sébastien Lenormand parachuted from the Montpelier Observatory in Paris.

Sébastien first used the word *parachute*. This French word means 'to shield a fall'.

Some early balloonists tried their parachutes out on dogs.

Others leapt from hot-air balloons.

An early parachute jump from a hot-air balloon

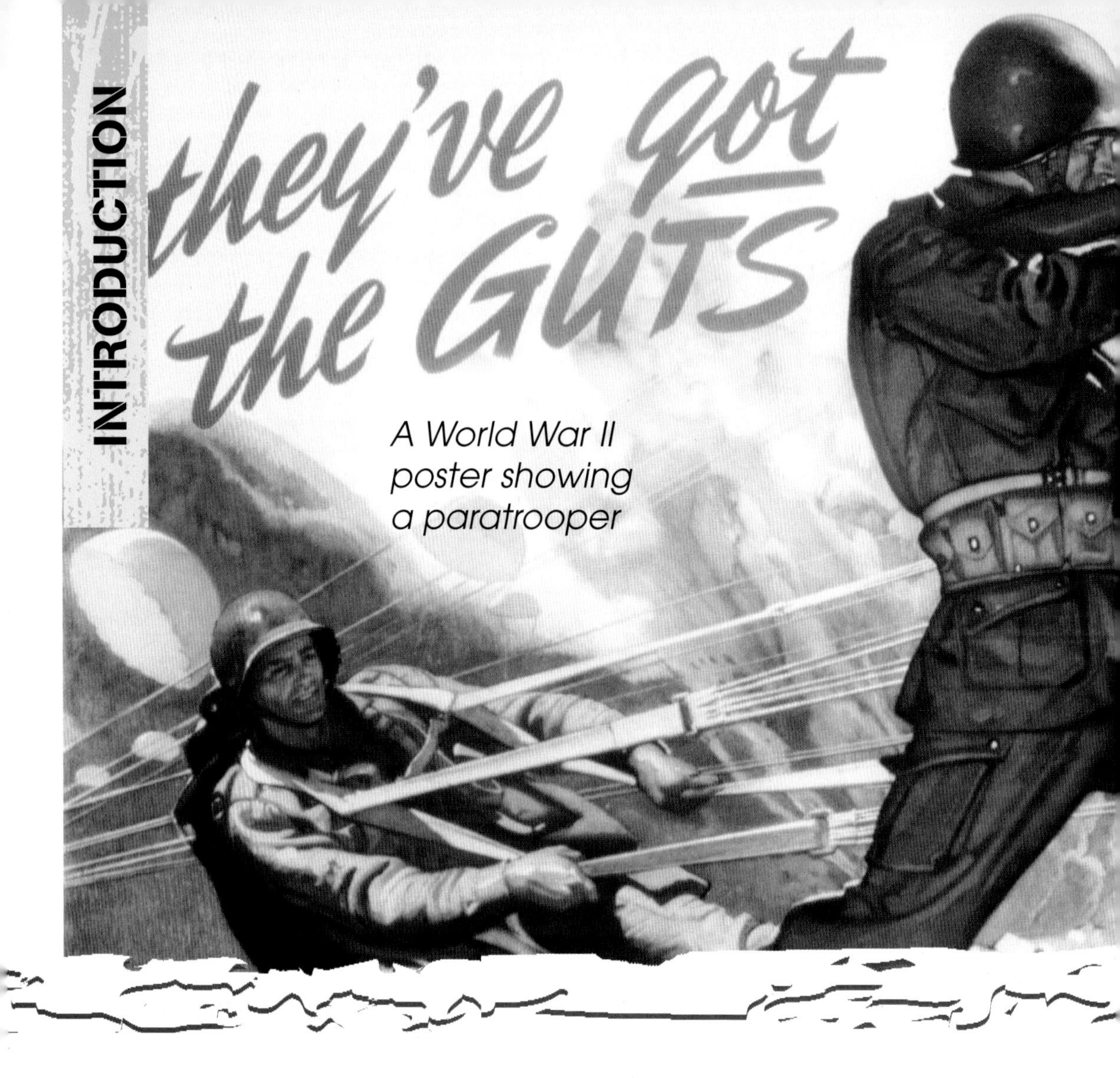

A World War II poster showing a paratrooper

THE FIRST FREE FALL

Until the 20th century, people thought you would black out in free fall. Georgia 'Tiny' Broadwick discovered this was untrue.

Tiny started parachuting in 1907 as a carnival act. She was only 14. Tiny went up attached to a balloon, released her parachute and floated down.

Leo Valentin

Militaries in other parts of the world began using parachutes.

The US Army added a second parachute in case the first failed.

Georgia 'Tiny' Broadwick

Kaethe Paulus designed a parachute for the German air force. In World War I, every German pilot was given one.

DEVELOPMENTS

In the 1950s, silk parachutes were given holes to create forward speed. This led to sport parachutes with a strange pattern of holes (see above).

Ram-air

In the 1950s, Domina Jalbert invented the ram-air – a rectangular parachute.

In the 1970s, the ram-air became the main parachute. Round parachutes were used as the reserve parachute.

In the 1980s, the ram-air design was used for reserves.

Originally ram-air parachutes had five-cells

A modern nine-cell ram-air parachute

Sport

By the 1990s, they became nine cells.

Many developments in parachuting took place in the 1990s. Parachuting is now a popular sport.

CHAPTER 2: ALL THE GEAR

Parachutes are lightweight, high performance and very reliable. Skydivers wear many high-tech gadgets to help to keep them safe.

GO FAST
JAVELIN

PARACHUTES

A modern ram-air parachute is inflated with air through the openings at the front, in the cells. These cells are closed at the back, so the parachute is stable.

A ram-air parachute has a forward speed of about 40–50 kilometres per hour. The forward speed keeps the canopy inflated.

A ram-air canopy is made from nylon and is covered with a special liquid.

Venezuelan pro Francisco Neri

Skydivers still use a reserve parachute.

The main and the reserve parachutes are packed together in one neat container.

Parachutes being packed. The main parachute is in a black bag above the reserve.

ACCESSORIES

Skydivers wear jumpsuits over their clothes. This stops loose material flapping over emergency handles.

Helmet

Helmets protect the head in case of collisions in the sky or hard landings.

Goggles protect the eyes from wind.

Goggles

Some people wear open-faced helmets with goggles instead of closed helmets.

Gloves

Thin leather gloves keep the hands warm, protect from line burns and give good grip.

Weights

Lighter jumpers wear lead weights so they fall faster. This helps them to fly in free fall at the same speed as heavier people.

Knife

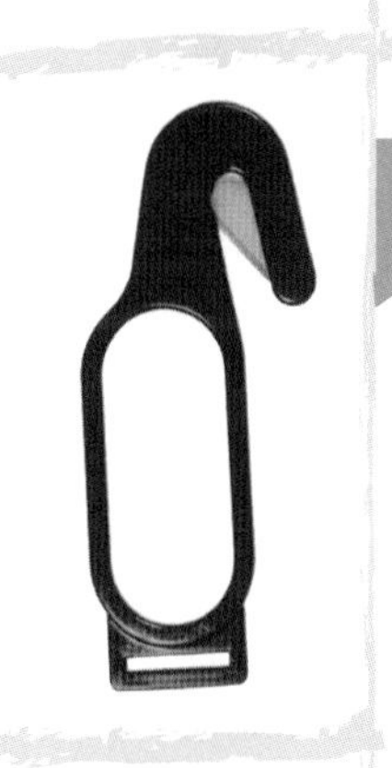

Skydivers often carry a knife to cut through lines in case they get tangled.

GADGETS

Cells

Each cell of the canopy is a different colour.

Brake lines

These connect the back of the canopy to the toggles.

Harness

The pilot is strapped into the harness. It is connected to the main and reserve parachutes.

Toggles

These are the brakes of the parachute. Toggles can also be used to steer.

Most skydivers wear an automatic activation device (ADD). This operates the reserve if the main parachute fails.

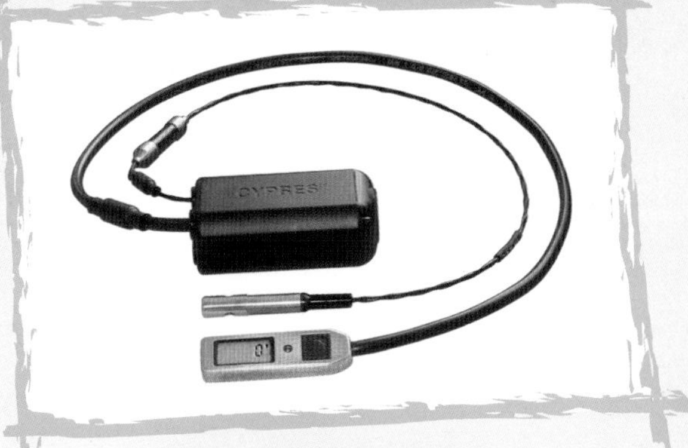

An automatic activation device

An altimeter shows the skydiver's height above the ground.

An altimeter

Recent technology includes a head-up display. The altitude and free-fall speed are projected into the view of the skydiver.

American Craig Girard with a head-up altitude display

CHAPTER 3: CANOPY FLIGHT

The world's top pilots can fly in formation, do a 360-degree turn and skim across the surface of a lake together!

A paraski competition

ACCURACY

In accuracy competitions, each jumper tries to land as close to the target as possible. This is a tiny circle, about the size of a man's thumbnail.

If you land on the disc, you score a zero. If you land further away, the distance is your score.

At world level accuracy competitions there is often a jump-off between two competitors to decide the winner.

Cheryl Stearns (USA)

Cheryl Stearns is the most successful competitive skydiver in the world.

She has been US Women's Accuracy Champion a record 22 times.

Vertical accuracy

In paraski competitions, entrants jump onto a ski slope and are scored for accuracy.

Then they slalom down a ski run and are scored on their times. The combined scores give the winner.

Extreme canopy piloting by Jay Moledzki (Canada)

CANOPY PILOTING

Canopy piloting competitions have three areas: speed, distance and zone accuracy. In speed, the canopy pilots are scored on how fast they go.

After the skydive, they open their canopies and fly in a series of spirals to build up speed.

Jonathan Tagle (USA)

Jonathan Tagle started skydiving at age 31, but he did 800 jumps in his first year. He has now completed over 5,000 jumps.

In 2005 he was overall world champion in canopy piloting.

Freestyle canopy piloting by Ian Bobo (USA)

Freestyle is creative canopy piloting. The pilot can create new artistic moves in the air.

CANOPY FORMATION

Single canopies can be linked together in many ways. You can join them on top of one another, side by side or you can combine the two methods and build amazing formations.

There are speed competitions where the aim is to join together the fastest.

A rotation (formation) competition team

The best way to build a large formation is in a diamond. A diamond is very stable.

The world record of a formation of 85 people was set in 2005.

81 canopies

CHAPTER 4: FREE FALL

Free fall is a unique experience. It does not feel like falling since you're not going past anything. The sensation is of flying.

THE STABLE POSITION

If you go into free fall curled up in a ball, you will tumble. But if you make your body streamlined, you can fly without spinning or rolling over. This is called the stable position.

The usual skydiving position is belly-to-earth, as shown above. The body acts like a shuttlecock.

In a free fall dive, you can reach 320 kilometres per hour!

A shuttlecock falling downwards; the arrows show the air flow.

Skydivers usually jump at 3,962 metres, free fall for one minute, then open their parachutes at 762 metres.

Stable position

Once you can fall in the stable position, it is easy to change the angle of your body to move it through the air.

FORMATION SKYDIVING

Joining together in free fall is called formation skydiving.

Speed

The simplest competition is speed. The winning team is the fastest to build a formation.

Teams

Teams contain four or eight people. They leave the aircraft linked together.

The British eight-way team

Claire 'Sparky' Scott

Claire is the only woman to have won five world titles in four-way formation skydiving.

Sparky gained her nickname by flying into power lines and cutting off electricity to a whole village!

British skydiver Claire 'Sparky' Scott

LARGE FORMATIONS

It is possible to build very large formations. The world record is 400 skydivers!

World record

Five enormous aircraft taking 80 people each were used for the world record. The jump was from 7,010 metres. The record included jumpers from 40 different countries.

Women's world record

Women have their own world record of 151 people, set in 2005 in California, USA.

Five Hercules planes load for the world-record attempt in 2006.

FREEFLYING

Flying in free fall in non-belly-to-earth positions is called freeflying.

Freefly competitions involve teams of three. One person wears a camera, and the other two skydivers perform together.

Judges score the routine on its technical and artistic content.

A totem: one freeflyer stands on another's shoulders

The head-down position is popular when freeflying because it is fast.

There is less free fall before it is time to go belly-to-earth and open the parachute.

The head-down position

HEAD-DOWN FORMATIONS

The head-down world record is 69 people, set in Chicago, USA, in 2007.

A head-down formation

Head-down world record 53-way in 2005

Eli Thompson (USA)

Eli Thompson

Eli Thompson has taken part in every head-down world record.

One of the inventors of freeflying, he started the Flyboyz team with two friends in 1996.

Yoko Okazaki and Axel Zohmann (Japan)

Okazaki and Zohmann

Husband and wife Yoko Okazaki and Axel Zohmann have a freestyle team called Axis 21. They hold two world records and many international medals.

CHAPTER 5: GETTING STARTED

There are proven safe ways to start skydiving. Here is someone on her second jump. The instructors are on guard on either side. This is called accelerated free fall (AFF).

TANDEM SKYDIVING

The three ways to start skydiving are tandem, AFF and static line.

A tandem jump is in a dual harness with an instructor.

A tandem parachute and harness is made for two. A complete beginner jumps with an instructor.

Tandems leave the aircraft at around 3,657 metres and free fall for 30 seconds.

A tandem instructor (top) and beginner (bottom)

In a tandem jump, the instructor opens the canopy at about 1,524 metres.

A tandem landing

ACCELERATED FREE FALL (AFF)

An AFF jump is with an instructor on either side in free fall.

The instructors communicate to the beginner with hand signals.

AFF jumps

The first AFF jump is from 3,657 metres with two instructors, one on either side.

The beginner opens the parachute at 1,524 metres.

Training

An AFF course takes one day of training. The full course is eight to ten jumps. The first three jumps are with two instructors. After that, there is only one instructor.

Qualifying

Every AFF course is adapted to suit the individual skydiver. Sometimes the jumps are videotaped.

STATIC LINE AND TUNNELS

A static-line jump is on your own. Adults can do a static-line jump from around 1,066 metres.

The static line is attached to the aircraft. It automatically opens the parachute.

Once the parachute has opened, the diver is talked down by radio.

The first free fall is five seconds.

First free fall

People who want to take up skydiving do another five to ten static-line jumps.

If these are good, they are cleared for their first AFF jump.

Wind tunnels

Vertical wind tunnels simulate free fall. Skydivers use them to practise competition routines.

They are fantastic if you want to learn to skydive.

A tunnel-flying skydiver

CHAPTER 6: EXTREME SKYDIVING AND STUNTS

This is Dutch pro skydiver Martijn van Dam jumping off a high-rise building.

World champion sky surfer Tanya Garcia-O'Brien (USA)

SKY SURFING

Sky surfers ride waves on surfboards thousands of metres up in the air.

Sky-surfing competition teams consist of a sky surfer and a camera flier.

Judges score the routine on creativity, originality and difficulty. Judges also score the filming.

Sky surfboards look like skateboards, but there are removable attachments for the feet.

A sky surfer with a boogie board

Sky-surfing time line

1980 – Skydivers in California, USA, first use boogie boards.

1987 – Frenchman Joel Cruciani stands up on a sky surfboard.

1989 – Patrick de Gayardon and Laurent Bouquet from France design an attachment-and-release system for the feet.

1997 – First world championships in sky surfing are held.

BASE JUMPING

Base jumping is skydiving from a fixed object.

Base jumping is more dangerous than normal skydiving. Jumpers do not use a reserve parachute and they can collide with the object they are jumping from.

Austrian Felix Baumgartner prepares to jump from the Christ the Redeemer statue in Rio de Janeiro, Brazil.

Climb to jump

Climbing the object is part of the adventure and gives a good workout before the jump.

Jumping off the Eiger Mushroom in Switzerland

The Pit of the Swallows has 80,000 birds living in it

Underground skydiving

A cave in Mexico allows skydivers to jump underground!

You have to fly in a constant spiral to avoid hitting the walls.

WING SUITS

We now have wing suits that double the free-fall time.

The modern birdman has one huge wing stretching from the wrists to the ankles. The large wing creates forward movement like a sail. The result is a long flight at a slow speed.

Flocks

Birdmen fly in formations called flocks. The wing suits double the free-fall time and they enjoy whizzing around the sky.

Adrian Nicholas

Longest free fall

It was using a wing suit from 9,144 metres that British skydiver Adrian Nicholas set a record for the longest free fall of four minutes 55 seconds in 1998.

STUNTS

In 1998, Belgian Bruno Brokken and German Richie Hornig flew their canopies under Besalu Bridge in Spain for the film *Crosswind*.

It took precise timing and control for the skydivers to avoid hitting the sides of the bridge.

Bruno Brokken

Dave Morris landing on the hot-air balloon

Balloon landing

In 2001, Briton Dave Morris skydived from a helicopter at 3,048 metres and opened his canopy. He landed on top of a hot-air balloon at 1,524 metres. Dave then jumped off the top of the balloon. He went into free fall for the second time in one skydive!

Adrian Nicholas and the da Vinci parachute

Da Vinci parachute

In 2000, Adrian Nicholas launched Leonardo da Vinci's 500 year-old parachute idea.

The da Vinci parachute was launched from a hot-air balloon at 3,048 metres over South Africa.

MILESTONES

1483 – Leonardo da Vinci sketches the first known parachute.

1783 – Frenchman Sébastien Lenormand jumps from the Montpelier Observatory, France, using a 4-metre-diameter frame parachute.

1785 – Frenchman Jean-Pierre Blanchard invents the first foldable parachute, made of silk.

1797 – André-Jacques Garnerin, from France, makes the first jump using a parachute without a rigid frame.

1837 – First parachuting death by Robert Cocking of England.

1890 – Germans Paul Letteman and Kaethe Paulus invent a backpack-type container and start using parachutes folded into bags.

Early parachuting world championship, 1981

1895 – Kaethe Paulus demonstrates a 'cutaway'. It releases one parachute before opening a second parachute.

1911 – First aeroplane jump, over Venice Beach, California, USA, by American Grant Morton.

1913 – American Georgia 'Tiny' Broadwick is the first woman to jump from an aeroplane.

1947 – Frenchman Leo Valentin invents the stable position.

1951 – Raymond Young, from the USA, first uses the term *skydiving*.

1960 – Highest parachute jump of 31,333 metres by American Colonel Joseph Kittinger in New Mexico, USA.

1998 – Longest free fall of four minutes 55 seconds by Briton Adrian Nicholas.

The 2006 world championship in canopy piloting in Vienna, Austria

GLOSSARY

Birdman Someone who skydives in a wing suit. An old-fashioned term for anyone who made wings and tried to fly.

Boogie board A short, light surfboard ridden lying face down.

Cells Each section of a ram-air canopy.

Cutaway Getting rid of the main canopy, usually when it has not opened properly or is tangled around something or someone.

Emergency handles These are located on the parachute harness for use if things go wrong.

Extreme canopy piloting Flying a parachute to gain maximum performance, usually making a complete spiral or two with the canopy to build up speed.

Formation Two or more jumpers linked in free fall (formation skydiving) or under a canopy (canopy formation).

Freefly To free fall any way other than belly-to-earth.

Lines Pieces of thin cord that attach the parachute to the harness, similar to guy lines on a tent.

Paratrooper A soldier trained in parachuting. Paratroopers were first used extensively in World War II by Germany.

Pilot The person controlling the parachute (or aircraft).

Ram-air An aerofoil parachute, open at the front and closed at the back. It is rammed full of air and becomes a solid flying wing. Its shape is rectangular but slightly curved.

Reserve A second parachute worn in case the first (main) parachute does not open properly.

Rotation One rotation is when the top person in a stack collapses his or her canopy, falls past everyone else and joins the stack at the bottom.

Slalom A ski race down a winding course marked by flags or poles.

Stack A formation where ram-air canopies are linked vertically above one another. The top jumper's feet are hooked into the bottom person's lines.

Static line A line attached to the aircraft that pulls the main parachute out and open as the jumper leaves the plane.

Wing suit A jumpsuit with fabric between the legs and arms. It increases lift and free-fall time.

INDEX